POSITIVE DISCIPLINE FOR PRESCHOOLERS

Positive Discipline for Preschoolers

Laying the Foundation for Raising a Capable, Confident Child Everyday Parenting Problems

G.P. Clifford

Amplitudo LTD

COPYRIGHT

© Copyright 2021 by Gerarld Paul Clifford. All right reserved.

The work contained herein has been produced with the intent to provide relevant knowledge and information on the topic described in the title for entertainment purposes only. While the author has gone to every extent to furnish up to date and true information, no claims can be made as to its accuracy or validity as the author has made no claims to be an expert on this topic. Notwithstanding, the reader is asked to do their own research and consult any subject matter experts they deem necessary to ensure the quality and accuracy of the material presented herein.

This statement is legally binding as deemed by the Committee of Publishers Association and the American Bar Association for the territory of the United States. Other jurisdictions may apply their own legal statutes. Any reproduction, transmission or copying of this material contained in this work without the express written consent of the copyright holder shall be deemed as a copyright violation as per the current legislation in force on the date of publishing and subsequent time thereafter. All additional works derived from this material may be claimed by the holder of this copyright.

The data, depictions, events, descriptions and all other information forthwith are considered to be true, fair and accurate unless the work is expressly described as a work of fiction. Regardless of the nature of this work, the Publisher is exempt from any responsibility of actions taken by the reader in conjunction with this work. The Publisher acknowledges that the reader acts of their own accord and releases the author and Publisher of any responsibility for the observance of tips, advice, counsel, strategies and techniques that may be offered in this volume.

CONTENTS

Copyright v
Introduction ix
I - Chapter 1: Positive Discipline 1
II - Chapter 2: Myths Of Toddler Discipline   17
III - Chapter 3: Filling Communication Gaps   28
IV - Chapter 4: Communicating With Your Toddler 43
V - Chapter 5: Compassion And Love . . . 58
VI - Chapter 6: Remaining Calm When You Don't Think You Can 72
VII - Chapter 7: School 82
VIII - Conclusion 98

INTRODUCTION

INTRODUCTION

Parenting is one job that does not come with a handbook or a supervisor to train you. While other parents may give you advice, it is up to you to choose how you will raise your child. This can be one of the hardest things you do in life because you will not know how well you did until your child is an adult. This book is here to give some more advice, tips, and tricks to raising your child using positive discipline.

The way you were raised may not be the best to raise your child. You could also have made the conscious decision not to raise your child in the same way. This book will give a fresh view on discipline that is meant to help your child become a well-rounded adult.

You may likely find that some things you thought were innocent can hurt a child in some way. For example, we will discuss the dangers of praise. Mind you, not all praise is bad, but excessive praise can end up hurting your child in the long run.

Some of the other things that will be discussed within the book include filling in communication gaps. I stand behind the belief that communication can be the solution to pretty much any problem in life. More often than not, children get in trouble because they did not know they were not supposed to do something. While the parent may have thought it was clear, the child did not. That is why communication is so important.

You will also learn how to focus on the strengths of your child instead of their weaknesses. This means that you let them know when they do well more often than you fuss at them for doing bad. This teaches them more of what they should do. They are more likely to behave correctly because they will not have to guess what they should do.

We will also go over the infamous power struggle that seems to happen between parent and child. You can diffuse a power struggle healthily, and this book will ensure your know-how.

We will talk about the importance of showing your child compassion and love and the importance of teaching them how to think versus what to think. If you are facing the teen years, we have got you covered as well. We will look at how disciplining a teen is different from a young child and the best way to face those struggles.

Lastly, we will go over how to work with your child's teacher so that they behave at home and at school. Often, children behave very differently at home than they do at school, sometimes better, sometimes worse. This will ensure that they behave properly in both places.

While I am not going to promise that the information within is one-size-fits-all, I will say that it can help make some of the tougher parenting moments easier. You also need to know your child, and some children need a more creative parenting approach. Let's begin.

1

CHAPTER 1: POSITIVE DISCIPLINE

CHAPTER 1: POSITIVE DISCIPLINE

Dr. Jane Nelsen created a discipline system that she names positive discipline. She based it on the works of Rudolf Deikurs and Alfred Adler. It was created to teach young children how to become resourceful, responsible, and respectful society members. This form of discipline can teach crucial life and social skills to encourage respect in adults and children.

Research has shown that children have been hardwired at birth to have a connection to others. Children who feel connected to their school, family, and community do not act out as often. If you want your child to be a contributing and successful member of their community, they have to learn the right life and social skills.

There are five criteria that you need to have to create positive discipline:

- You have to be both firm and kind at the same time
- You have to help your child feel like they are significant and belong
- You have to make sure the discipline will work long-term
- You need to make sure that you teach them valuable life and social skills so they can create good character traits like cooperation, contribution, accountability, problem-solving, concern for others, and respect
- Invite your child to figure out how capable they are and how to use their powers constructively

Positive discipline is meant to create mutually respectful relationships. It can teach adults ways to be firm and kind while it will not be permissive or punitive.

Some of the concepts and tools include:

- Mutual respect: You as an adult can model firmness by respecting yourself and what the situation needs. You model firmness when you respect the child's needs
- Find the belief that causes the behavior: To effectively discipline a child, you have to be able to recognize why a child does what they do and then help them change these beliefs instead of just trying to change their behaviors
- Effective problem solving and communication skills
- The discipline needs to teach and is not punitive or permissive
- Focus on solutions rather than punishment
- Encouragement: When you encourage your child, you are noticing their efforts and improvements and not just on their successes. This helps build long-term empowerment and self-esteem.

Positive discipline also has some unique characteristics, and these include:

- Helping students and adults learn by doing experiments. This creates an opportunity for them to have fun learning and practice their new skills.
- Parent educational programs and classroom programs that stay consistent. Childcare workers, teachers, and parents need to work together to create a consistent and secure environment for the child.
- The training is very inexpensive, and it constantly supports the community members to teach everyone about positive discipline skills.
- It has certified teachers throughout the country that works with communities and schools.

The History

As stated above, positive discipline was based on Rudolf Dreikurs and Alfred Adler's works. Alfred Adler introduced this idea to audiences across the US during the 1920s. He advised that we needed to treat children with respect but stated that pampering and spoiling children should never be encouraged as this could cause behavioral and social problems. These classroom techniques were first used in Vienne during the early years of the 1920s, and Rudolf Drikurs brought these methods to the United States during the later part of the 1930s. Adler and Dreikurs referred to this new firm and kind approach to parenting and teaching as being a democratic approach.

During the '80s, Jane Nelsen and Lynn Lott went to a workshop that John Taylor was doing. Lynn started training others to teach about what they had learned, and with her interns helping her, they wrote the first "Teaching Parenting Manual." At the time, Jane had become the director of the ACCEPT Project. This is a federal project that received great status while it was still just in its development stage. She then wrote "Positive Discipline," that she then self-published in 1981. This book would then be published in 1987 by Ballantine. In 1988, Lynn and Jane collaborated on a book that has been titled "Positive Discipline for Teenagers." They started teaching classroom management and parenting skills from what they had learned. Jane and Lynn wrote another book called "Positive Discipline in the Classroom," and they created a manual full of activities for students and teachers.

Since then, the "Positive Discipline" books have been expanded to include things that look into the various age groups, family situations, and special situations. This is now being taught to parent educators, parents, and schools by people who have been certified by the "Certified Positive Discipline Associates." Teachers, parents, and community members are encouraged to be certified and share the positive discipline concepts within their own communities and groups.

These education classes are being taught worldwide and are being used successfully in the classroom and in public elementary, religious, and private school settings. They are currently developing a demonstration school program.

Why It Works

Evaluations that compare schools that use other forms of discipline with schools that use positive discipline are just starting. But studies about implementing positive disciples have shown that these tools can give great results. One study done in classrooms in low-income elementary schools over four years showed that vandalism decreased, suspensions decreased, and teachers said the classroom's academic performance, attitudes, behavior, and atmosphere improved significantly. Another study was done with teachers and parents who taught problem students. They started using the positive discipline method and found that it positively impacted the students' behaviors compared to a control school. Other studies that examined how positive discipline can impact children have all seen amazing results. Studies keep showing that when a student feels like they are a part of the school, it decreases risky behaviors like suicidal thoughts and emotional distress while increasing their academic performance. There is a lot of scientific proof that teaching children proper social skills can have a protective impact that is going to last the child throughout their life. Students who have been taught these social skills succeed better in school and will not get caught up in problematic behaviors.

Even though studies have been done about the positive discipline program, it is still considered in its early stages. While this may be true, similar programs have been studied for a longer time and are just as effective in changing behaviors. In one study done on teenagers' parents, they discovered that parents were not as oppressive with the decisions they made and could do effective problem-solving. Positive discipline helps parents gain the skills they need to be firm yet kind. Several studies have shown that teens who think of their parents as being firm and kind do not normally take up habits like becoming sexually active, being violent, using alcohol, using marijuana, or smoking. Other studies show that when a teen perceives their parent is firm and kind, they will have better academic performance.

Alfred Adler was a psychiatrist from Vienna who came to America. Even though he worked with Freud, he had different views of human behaviors. Adler thought that past events did not drive a child's behavior but moved toward a common goal of belonging that influenced every person's decision that they make about the world, others, and themselves. Rudolf Dreikurs was also a psychiatrist from Vienna. He was the director of a child guidance center located in Vienna. This center would use Adler's ways in the classroom and with the families. Dreikurs fled Vienna to avoid persecution from the Nazis during 1937. Dreikurs is considered to be one of the first people who noticed how beneficial group therapy could be for people. He also advocated for relationships being based upon mutual respect before home life and school life. He has written some well-known books that include "*The Psychology of the Classroom,*" "*Maintaining Sanity in the Classroom,*" and "*Children the Challenge.*"

A Great Way to Get Children to Behave

If you were to ask 1000 parents to tell you their least favorite part about parenting, you would probably hear discipline the most. But having a good discipline foundation is crucial to help prevent parents from experiencing burnout. The majority of parents who have been relying on traditional punishment methods will tell you that they feel guilty, horrible, and exhausted each day after they have had to face a day of nagging, lecturing, and yelling. They feel disconnected from themselves and their child. They would like to be able to do things differently. This is where positive discipline comes into play.

Positive discipline is a philosophy that has been based on mutual respect, empowerment, and encouragement. It will support that parent and help them find solutions for their child's misbehavior instead of using punishment. Discipline is concerned with guiding children and gets rid of the need for being punitive or permissive.

Taking care of your children relies heavily on communication as the parent has to explain everything to their child. They have to tell their child about the unwanted behaviors they need to work on, why they have to work on it, and the consequences. As the parent, you have to keep a firm but warm tone, and you need to encourage your children to make the best choices they can that will work for them.

This technique involves encouraging the behaviors you want to see while discouraging actions that you want them to give up. It does not matter what you are doing; above all, you have to keep your feelings under control. You cannot get mad when you feel frustrated. It does not matter if you are trying to decrease or increase a behavior; you have to keep a respectful, positive relationship with your child.

This is a lot easier said than done, but it might help if you can help your child figure out their feelings or give them a choice. A good option would be to say, "I know you want to continue playing, but it is bath time. Would you like to leave your toy right here to take it to the bath? It is up to you." You could also say something like this: "It is okay to feel frustrated, but it is not okay to bite, throw things, kick, or hit. What words could you use to tell me what you need?" By doing this, children will feel more empowered. It also helps teach them to make better options.

Does Negative Discipline Exist?

When talking about parenting philosophy, no. Nobody purposefully subscribes to negative discipline. However, there are certain types of discipline that can have a negative impact, like giving them the "silent treatment," guilt-tripping, spanking, or yelling. This type of discipline might work for a little bit, but it has some very bad consequences for your child's development.

Anytime a parent uses any of these methods, your child will be more focused on your anger rather than what you are trying to teach them. Plus, it is hard for your child to manage their emotions respectfully and effectively when they are not being shown how to regulate their emotions. Children who are treated to nothing but negative discipline are usually more aggressive, anxious, and depressed. They will likely struggle in school and socially. Punishment only lets them know the things they should not be doing, but positive discipline helps them learn the things they should be doing in a respectful, empowering, and kind manner Positive discipline provides you with better ways to find solutions to your child's behavior instead of just temporarily stopping the problems.

Positive Discipline Works

That statement is true, especially in the long run. Studies have found that kids act better when they experience get to see kindness and firmness from the parents and the teachers. If a child can see that their caregivers respond to how they feel and what they need while keeping their high expectations, the child normally does not engage in the same type of risky actions, and they are going to find more success at school and in society. They will find it much easier to reach their goals in life, and they will be more motivated to succeed if they have parents who are firm and loving.

It Does Take Practice and Time

This is very true for those who had parents who were permissive or authoritarian because their styles did not involve the same amount of communication as a positive discipline. They must be offered the correct type of rewards. This type of discipline makes you use verbal rewards along with services, goods, privileges, or gifts. You have to be careful with non-verbal awards because it could unintentionally turn into bribery. We all know that this will not help them create an internal sense of self-awareness and responsibility. When you use positive discipline, you must do frequent check-ins to make sure you are sticking with the program. Children tend to want to find the cracks in life naturally

Starting Positive Discipline

There are certified trainers that hold workshops and classes all over the country.

Look at the way your family handles their feelings. The first thing you have to learn to do is to listen more often. If a kid feels significant and belongs, they will not act out as often and will cooperate and listen better. It is important to understand that kids learn how they should regulate and manage emotions by watching adults regulate and managed their emotions. We have to learn how to model the behavior that we want to see in our children.

Talk to your child's teachers. Positive discipline is

now being used at times in classrooms to help manage the behavior of the class. This can happen anytime a teacher is firm and warm, and they provide their students with clear expectations as to what they need to do. They will offer them clear guidelines for behaviors that are not acceptable. They will help to work with their students to ensure they can find helpful solutions to their problems. They also reward positive behaviors and changes that they see and discourage negative actions transparently and clearly so that there is no confusion. If a teacher can do this in a classroom with 20 plus students, you can do it at home with yours.

Create a family goal and talk about a plan for ways to reach it. Do not forget to give them a lot of choices.

Positive Discipline Examples

You are ready to begin using positive discipline in your home but unsure how to get started and keep reading. Here are four strategies that you can implement:

- Redirection

Young children have an extremely short attention span, so it really is not all that hard to redirect them to a different activity when they begin acting out. If your child is playing with something that might be dangerous, find another toy that you know they enjoy playing with to take their attention off of the dangerous one. If this does not work, take them into a different room or take a walk outside.

If your child is older, you can just tell them what to do instead of what they can't. Instead of telling them that they can't watch television, give them a choice of either going outside to play or working on a puzzle. If you can remain focused on the positive, it could reduce defiant behavior and arguments.

• Positive Reinforcement

If your child does something good, give them some praise. If they share their favorite toy with their friend, tell them they are very generous. If they show kindness to others, tell them they did a great job.

This gives them positive attention for all the things they are doing right, instead of reinforcing everything they did wrong. If your child breaks a rule, you can explain ways that they can make better choices at other times.

• Stop Using Time Outs

Giving your child a time out can be effective, but it

has been used to death. When you place your child in time outs constantly, it might backfire and make them act out more because they are trying to get your affection and attention.

If your child does misbehave, sit them down and talk to them about what they did wrong instead of just putting them in time out. Try reading them their favorite book and do this until they have calmed down and are ready to apologize for how they behaved.

· One-Word Reminders

Instead of demanding that your child does something like sharing their toys, putting their coat away, or stop running; just say one word in a normal tone like share, coat, or walk. Giving them gently reminders will not get defensive, but they will remember the right behavior.

There might be times when you have to choose your battles. Some people might look at this as having a lack of discipline rather than a discipline method. You have to use it wisely.

You will exhaust your child and yourself if you are constantly telling them to do other things or redirect them.

If it is a minor problem, it may be worth your sanity just to ignore it. If there is a way you can prevent this behavior, like putting something out of their reach, do it when the situation has passed.

You have to use this carefully, but it can create a relaxed atmosphere if you realize your household is becoming too tense. If your child normally acts out just to get attention, it is going to tell the child that you will not always respond to them. The main belief of positive discipline is there are not any bad children, only bad behaviors.

II

CHAPTER 2: MYTHS OF TODDLER DISCIPLINE

CHAPTER 2: MYTHS OF TODDLER DISCIPLINE

There is probably not another area of life that is filled with more myths than parenting and discipline. Parents have been trying to control their child's actions for millennia. This impulse has given a mix of results. Frantic parents have dreamed up numerous discipline methods, and they get the stamp of approval by some who think they work, and they soon become cultural norms. However, received wisdom is not necessarily wisdom. Often, they are hand-me-down myths.

When talking about discipline, they are most often the more pernicious and prominent of the bunch. As if it wasn't hard enough to raise a child, now we have to figure out if our discipline methods are myth or fact. Fear not, for we shall go over those myths now. Don't be surprised if you see a lot of discipline strategies that were used on you or that you may have used on your child. Also, don't worry if you have used some of them. You can stop and prevent any lasting problems.

Myth #1: Spanking Never Hurt Anybody

We're getting this one out of the way first because it is likely the most controversial and well-known discipline method out there. Spanking has become less common practice, but there are still those who believe in corporal punishment. In 2014, a study found that 76% of men and 65% of women agreed that it was okay to spank their child. This is despite the fact that there is overwhelming evidence from experts that explain that this disciplinary tactic is completely ineffective and is more often counterproductive.

One study, published in 2016 in the *Journal of Family Psychology,* studied more than 50 years of research that was linked to more than 160,000 children who had been disciplined by being spanked in some fashion. Using the meta-analysis, the researchers discovered that spanking rarely altered the child's bad behavior over the long-term. However, they found that it did correlate with antisocial tendencies, aggression, and poor mental health. What's worse is that the outcomes were almost identical to the consequences of childhood abuse.

Even if you are a parent who only spanks once in a blue moon, and you don't spank them regularly, it may not have long-term damage, but it can change in a moment. If you are an occasional spanker, there is a chance that when you do spank, you will up the ante and hit harder when the spanking doesn't work to stop their behavior. Parents should want their child to feel comfortable coming to you when they need, and to make sure they aren't afraid of you. Kids will do something wrong. That's human nature. But through the occasional spank, all you are doing is making your kid afraid of coming to you and learning better ways to hide their bad behavior.

Experts have long asked parents to quit spanking, even if they received spankings as children and "turned out fine." Physical contact can be an extremely powerful tool, but when things start to get heated between you and your child, instead of going for a paddle, try getting on your child's level and disarming them through gentle touch, like a hug, so that they can focus and be brought back into the moment.

Myth #2: Shouting to Get Their Attention Is Fine

When your child's actions of gone off the charts, it can seem like they have crawled into chaotic space. Since you can't shake them to get them to come back to the real world, the most obvious alternative would be to shout at them, right?

No.

As it turns out, to stop your child's behavior, it is better to get close to them and get quiet. This is because, at some point in their life, the yelling will become normalized. Your child will start to think that is how people talk, but when you get quiet, your child can't hear you until they quit screaming. And, trust me, they will stop screaming and making a fuss.

Parenting experts also tell us the calm needs to come along with quiet. Frustration and anger only form a feedback loop of emotion. That doesn't help things in the home, and it definitely won't look good when walking through a grocery store. When your use clam close-talking, you will teach them how to be calm.

Myth #3: Strict Parenting Creates Well-Behaved Children

There is this notion that the only way you can have a good child is to be hard on them all the time. However, this all-or-nothing parenting style does not encourage a child to develop any form of empathy or emotional intelligence. This is because their parents aren't modeling that type of thing for them.

Even a former Marie drill sergeant understands that it's unproductive to make demands of small children. Master Sergeant Chris Lopez explains that redirection and explanation will give you a better outcome. He has learned to avoid conflicts in the home by using patience and a lot of talking about why things happen.

A common method of discipline with strict parenting is the famous "Because I said so" line. When you are authoritarian, you are going to either raise a rigid child who is afraid of you that doesn't do anything out of fear of what you will do, or a child who becomes rebellious and has oppositional issues because they don't feel heard or seen.

Myth #4: Saying Yes Means You Failed

This idea that yes means you fail likely comes from the idea that a parent doesn't have boundaries with their child. That's simply not true.

When telling your child yes, there will be a reasonable strategy to keep from creating an unnecessary conflict that will force a parent into a discipline strategy that hasn't been thought through. The main concern of a parent is always the health and safety of their child. After all, you have a small human with an underdeveloped prefrontal cortex struggling with the desires.

As a parent, you can use your child's desires to achieve your desired outcome by saying "yes." The most important thing is to make sure that your yes is connected with a condition. Instead of completely giving in to them, you would say, "Yes, when," or "Yes, if." Your child will then have to meet that condition to get what they asked for. The important thing to remember is that the condition needs to be somewhat related to the request, and you need to provide them with a brief explanation as to why they have to meet the condition.

It also works like this. Saying, "Yes, you want to go to the party, and I'm not letting you, and I understand that's hard," will help your child's brain to move into an open state. On the other hand, saying, "No, you aren't going anywhere because you're not allowed to do that sort of thing," will cause them to go into a defensive state. This can create an argument.

Myth #5: You Should Never Negotiate With Your Child

There are ways to negotiate with your child that provide a better outcome. The main thing is that your child isn't the one holding all of the cards, even though they do feel as if they are. Parents need to use hostage negotiator tactics of empathy to create a connection with the child at the moment. It isn't all that difficult to acknowledge the difficulty of waiting for a cookie. Everybody has a hard time when it comes to waiting for a treat they like.

Then you have to provide them with a wide array of acceptable options. Parents are always in control of the terms of the negotiation, but the child will suddenly feel as if they are in control because you have provided them with the chance to make a choice. Little do they know that they are doing what you want them to do.

While the child sees it as negotiation, it's really just manipulation on the parent's part. It's not a myth that this type of discipline does always work.

Myth #6: The Terrible Twos are Terrible

The feeling that this time in your child's life is more terrible than any other time is personal. This time isn't actually terrible. It's all about developmentally appropriate expectations of what a two-year-old can do. It's all about noticing their needs, labeling them, and then naming them for the child so that they can understand things. At this time, they are struggling to understand what is going on, and that's why they get upset. This labeling process also helps to set limits and boundaries.

This is the time when a child is learning how to control their emotions, which aren't fully developed. When you look at it in this light, it gives you a different view of the situation. This can help you remain calm in the most stressful moments.

Myth #7: After Three, Their Brain is "Set" For Life

This is all based on the power of the early years of life. It's remarkable that the brain forms a million or more neural connections per second during those first few years of life. That doesn't mean their brain is set after the first three years. What is true is that the brain does grow drastically during those first few years, but it can still change for a long time.

Myth #8: Sugar Makes Kids Hyper

This is a very common myth, but studies have now

found that the parent's perception of how their child is going to act after eating sugar is what causes the child to get hyper. It's a self-fulfilling prophecy. The more you believe that your child is going to get hyper, the greater chance they will become hyper. While sugar isn't all that healthy for your child to have a lot of, it is not linked to hyperactivity.

Myth #9: You Should Shield Your Child from Loss

This could be a question to go over because any parent would prevent loss for their child if they had to so that they never had to experience any traumatic or horrible things. However, if you pretend those things don't exist or try to shield them from information about those things they will find out about, you prevent them from building resilience. They need to build resilience, and they do that by experiencing loss and then having the support of loved ones to help them get through it.

That's why it's important to be straightforward with them lovingly and sensitively and explain the loss to them. A child who is told that their dog ran away instead of their dog died will stop trying to work through the loss and could spend days, weeks, or years fixated on waiting for their dog to come back.

It's healthier to sit with them and support them through difficult situations as they happen.

Myth #10: Parents Who Are Committed and Attached to Their Child Will Have Kids Who Behave Properly

A parent can be completely committed to their child from birth. You could make sure you do everything perfectly. In fact, you might just be a faultless saint, and a child is still going to misbehave. Every single child is going to misbehave. Children are going to make mistakes. They are all going to have a temper tantrum, fuss, and whine. This is all about the developmental process.

The reality is, all you can do is love your child and do the best you can. Don't allow what is normal misbehavior to affect your confidence as a parent. Give your child and yourself enough room to be a normal human.

Myth #11: Parenting Should Come Naturally

Loving a child is easy. Raising them is hard. Being an effective parent is a learned skill, not something that just happens. Parenting will present some intense, complicated, and ever-changing situations. To be an effective parent, you are going to need certain skills and knowledge, but nobody is born with that information.

It's a lot like driving a car or learning any type of hobby or sport; good parenting is something we have to learn. This can be done through trial-and-error, but that can be extremely frustrating. Instead, you can join a support group, take a class, or read a book.

There is a lot of stress placed on parents, especially in a world with social media. Everybody, even those who aren't parents, think they know what's best. All you have to do is look at celebrity moms and see how they are "mom-shamed" for doing something that is pretty much insignificant. You should think about these myths and replace them with your own truth. This can help you approach parenting more enjoyably, reducing your chance of clashing with your toddler or creating problems you will have to deal with later on.

ID

CHAPTER 3: FILLING COMMUNICATION GAPS

CHAPTER 3: FILLING COMMUNICATION GAPS

Parenting is a beautiful but demanding journey. You are in parenthood the moment your child is conceived, and it goes on until the end of life. Parents are models that children learn to imitate throughout their childhood. If parents pay attention to their child's ideas and concerns, it will teach them that they are an important member of the family. Communication between children and parents is the heart of teaching these future adults effective communication with other people. Children will learn behaviors, values, attitudes, and knowledge by communicating with others, and the most important person is their parents. They are communicating with your child starts the day your child is born, or even earlier if you are like me. I talked to my daughter while she was still in the womb. This communication has to continue while the child grows, changes, and matures.

Patterns within the communication will change as your child hits adolescence as their peers become the most important people in their life even though positive communication will lead to poor communication, feelings of worth, cooperation, and nurturing relationships. In contrast, poor communication could lead to children who have feelings of worthlessness while constantly bickering and fighting with their parents. When a child is young, they will share everything with their parents, but as the go through their teenage years, their friends turn into their confidants. The communication gap might be due to some differences in the people's perspectives and values that come from the generation gap that exists, along with being hesitant to openly talk with their parents about what is happening in their lives.

Encouraging Open Communication

Below you will find ways to openly encourage your child to communicate with you to fill the communication gap.

Take the Initiative

Begin any conversation to convey a message that you are interested in what they have to say. You could show that you are interested in what is happening in your child's life. Let them know that you respect their privacy, but they should know they can talk to you about anything in their life. Try your best to talk about private things like a specific behavior that you do not like or an incident that made you angry. Make sure you have your emotions under control before you begin talking to them. NEVER embarrass your child or make them the center of attention if you are around other people. If you notice something that really bothers you and you cannot refrain from pointing it out, go into another room and call your child to you and then talk about what you didn't like. This will be easier for them to understand rather than you blurting it out and embarrassing them in front of their friends.

Pay Attention

If your child wants to talk to you, you have to pay attention to them. It is easy to know when your child wants you to listen to them, like if they start talking during dinner, at bedtime, etc. There are different ways that you will tell your child that you are really listening to them. You can turn off the television, put down the newspaper, put down your cell phone, and look them in the eye while they are talking to you.

It Is Fine If You Are Tired

If you are too tired, tell them so. It does not take any effort, but they must understand that you are an active listener. This is needed if you want to be mindful of your child. If you tell your child that you are tired and ask them if you can talk later, this keeps you from forcing yourself to sit through a conversation that you will not follow.

Help Them Solve Their Problems

If you think you have to help fix a specific behavior, help them by showing them steps to the solution rather than putting down your child or just using words. If your child spends too much time on the phone and uses the excuse of having to stay connected to their friends, but their schoolwork is going downhill, you can bring this to their attention by talking about the problem that needs to be fixed. You can show them how much time they are spending on the phone and then give them a consequence if their schoolwork does not improve, they will lose their phone privileges. You can help them make a schedule so they can divide their time equally between chores, schoolwork, and other activities. This will help give them the confidence they need to make the right choices in life as they get older. This shows them that you want to help them and you want to take care of them.

Stay Away From Interruptions

If your child is talking to you and telling you about their day, do not interrupt them and ask them other questions. If they get home late, ask them if they are okay rather than just pointing out that they are late for curfew. Do not preach at them, do not talk down to them, and keep moralizing at a minimum as these things can hinder open communication. These kinds of interruptions will only make them wonder if you really do have their best interests in mind or if they can really rely on you to help them through their problems.

Encourage Communication

Letting your child know that you are happy that they chose to talk to you rather than them just going to their friends shows that they trust you. You can share your life experiences with them if it can help them with their problems. This lets them know that you know what you are talking about.

If You Make A Mistake, Own It

Apologizing anytime you are wrong can help your

child get more confidence in communicating openly with you since this shows them that they are not the only ones who have to apologize when they do something wrong.

When Did Talking With Your Child Get So Hard?

You should not have to get a doctorate in human relations plus ten years of debate team experience to communicate with your child. There might be a time when your child makes it feel that way. You can blame your way of parenting, social media, or MESD (multiple electronic screen disorder), but the social landscape for children has changed. This leaves us to cross a bridge that seems way more complicated than any bridge that we crossed as a child. In all reality, the path from a parent's question to a child's answer has not ever been completely straight.

Does this sound familiar?

You: "How did you get that bruise?"

Child: "I got it at school during recess."

You: "What happened?"

Child: "We were playing at recess."

The child picks up the remote control and increases the volume.

You: "Yes, but what happened? Did you get hurt playing?"

Child: "No."

You: "Did somebody hurt you on purpose?"

Child: "No, we were just playing."

You: "I thought you said that you did not get hurt playing?"

The child turns the volume up a few more notches.

Child: "No, that is not what I meant."

You: "Can you turn the volume down for a few minutes?"

Child: "Okay. Wait. Okay. This part is so funny. Okay, wait."

You: "Did you just tell me okay, or did you just tell me to wait?"

During the 1980s, Elaine Mazlish and Adele Faber took all of their experiences working with parenting groups, added in some perspectives from Haim Ginot, and wrote the book "*How to Talk So Kids Will Listen & Listen So Kids Will Talk.*" The book spoke to parents a very obvious message: we have to support and affirm our children's needs if we want them to stop making the same communication mistakes. Think about the conversation above, and you just want an explanation for the bruised leg that makes some sort of sense. Your questions seem clear, but the child never tells a story you can understand. Your response was just to ask more questions. Getting to the bottom of the story is what you want, right? What you are not getting is the meaning of the behavior. You are not engaging your child emotionally, and your child remains distant. Some people's first response to this is: "the child is rude. They need to respect their parent and turn off the television when he is being talked to." Maybe you should have chosen to focus on your child's manners, but the true story of what happened would have been lost forever.

Texture of Talk

Communicating with a child is a complex blend of behaviors, words, and emotional signals. Our pattern of communication has been set before a child can even speak words. There is a specific type of language that parents will use that researchers call "motherese." This shows up in parent's communications before the child learns to talk. "Motherese" is a language that represents both emotional and relational language. It is also training the baby to listen for phonetic sounds along with breaks between sentences and words. If a mother says: "All done, baby's all done." She will alternate between low and high tones that can help the baby's brain know they are separate sounds that have different meanings. At this moment, the child and parent are communicating together. They have a rhythm that will build an emotional bond between them while building the child's language skills. So what happens after the language learning job is finished? Why does this beautiful tango from their early childhood turn into an awkward two-step with every person constantly stepping on the other one's toes?

During their development, there comes a certain point that we put more emphasis on being more social rather than emphasizing the emotional tone in our conversations. The topics start revolving around the behaviors that we would like for our children to develop.

Look at this conversation:
You: "You should call your grandmother. She would love to hear about how well you did at your recital."
Child: "Seriously? She always sounds like she wants to get off the phone."
You: "That's just because she is worried about the long-distance charges. It is something that we used to have to worry about."
Child: "Can't I call her later? I'm looking up some new songs right now."
You: "The problem is that you never call you later, she has not heard your voice since last summer. That's been almost a year."

This communication breaks down when the parents emphasized the responsibility of a grandchild having to call their grandparents. Still, they do not connect the emotional dots of calling your grandparent is a way to love them.

Most of the time, parents will close the doors on communication in a way that seems obvious once they have been pointed out to us. It can be a challenge to see what we do in the moments, but here are some examples of communication breakers:

- Trying to Repeat Your Point Constantly

When you are constantly repeating your point over and over during a conversation, you are not getting your point across like you thought you were. "I do not know why I always have to tell you this, but..." This communication style comes from worrying that your child will not accept whatever point you are trying to make. With this type of dialogue, the parent only focuses on persuading their child and not communicating with them.

- Pointing Out HOW Your Child Is Talking While They are Talking

It is crucial to correct how your child communicates, but it does not need to be done while the child is expressing their feelings, even if it is a negative feeling about things. "Yes, you have to go with me to the bank, and please do not use that whiny voice when you are talking to me."

• Asking Why Too Much

"Why do you not want to sign up for baseball? You loved playing it last year." Nothing will shut down a conversation with a child quicker than asking questions about their "I do not know" response; when you ask a child "why," you are just telling them that they haven't realized that they are wrong. The child might be wrong, but when you try to knock down every statement that your child makes by asking them "why," it is wrong to do a thing. Keep in mind that children are the best imitators and will begin to ask you "why" in return when you try to tell them "no" when they ask for another scoop of ice cream.

• Showing Them That You are Getting Frustrated

The tone of your voice will tell your child that you are getting frustrated with them. "I have told you why we have to stop at the store." Yes, your child can frustrate you. Everyone gets frustrated, and we give it back to them, they will, in turn, give it back to us. This kind of communication is called ping-ponging, and it only escalates the negative emotions rather than getting rid of them.

The above are just examples of how we undermine our efforts to talk with our children while trying to help them learn how to communicate honestly and genuinely with other people. Learning new ways to communicate is not hard; all you have to do is take one step at a time and stop demanding that you never make mistakes.

Five Reasons There Is a Communication Gap

We have already established that there is a communication gap between children and parents. A child's development depends on healthy communications between the child and parents. Still, when you think about all the advances of technology and our fast-paced life, this communication gap has widened extremely. If parents continue scolding or nagging their children without showing any interest in them, children will lose interest in trying to talk to them. Some parents work overtime, come home completely exhausted, and get too busy to spend the right about of time with their children. Let's look at the fine biggest reasons behind the communication gap between children and parents.

Unnecessary Control

When parents think they have total control over their children, they will pressure them to make the best grades while ignoring their hobbies and interests. This kind of inflexible thinking suppresses the child's freedoms, and this makes them feel trapped. Because of this, children think their parents do not support their choices, and they start being secretive. They will not share their problems anymore.

Technological Gap

These days children are more tech-savvy than their parents. Parents do not always have the time to learn and handle the ever changing world of technology. Because of this, they do not stay updated with all the trends in their teenager's world. Having parental control software and not having digital knowledge can cause many misunderstandings between children and their parents. They also are not aware of all the sites that their children can access, and they can't monitor their child's online behavior that is an absolute must in today's society.

Insufficient Communication

If you take into consideration the heavy workload and stress that parents are under, parents might find it hard to find the time for their children. They don't spend a lot of time communicating, much less listening to their children because of their long hours. Due to this, children stay away from sharing their school life or events with parents because they feel neglected. These factors create large communication barriers between parent and child.

Different Perspectives and Attitudes

Many parents don't encourage new thoughts and ideas from their children. They try to impose their narrow thinking on their children. The parent just adopts a straight face, and they don't reflect their feelings while communicating with their children. Plus, they scream and yell at their child, and then they physically punish the child. Constant scolding and nagging just make the child more irritated. Parents don't see things from their child's point of view, which causes even larger gaps.

Unrealistic Expectations

Every parent has expectations and hopes for their child. Even though these might inspire a child to do better, having unrealistic ones will make them feel insecure, eventually taking its toll. When parents pressure and nag their children, children will feel inadequate when they can't meet these targets that their parents have set. This will lead to extremely low self-esteem, and they will begin criticizing themselves.

Even though it isn't easy to solve a child and parent's problems, it could be easily torn down if parents will just try to talk to their child each day. It is great to analyze the situation and then learn how to react healthily to avoid punishment and confrontations. Create some family activities like a fun trip, a picnic, or spend some quality time with the family. Parents need to give their children some space, so they feel comfortable sharing their problems.

IV

CHAPTER 4: COMMUNICATING WITH YOUR TODDLER

CHAPTER 4: COMMUNICATING WITH YOUR TODDLER

Talking to your child does many important things. Talking helps improve the bond you have with them while simultaneously encouraging them to listen to you. It can help them build self-esteem and form relationships.

Just like any other thing in life, listening and talking can be done ineffectively or effectively. Like with every other skill, your listening skills can get better the more your practice them.

To communicate well with your child, you have to make sure you do the following:

- Focus on actions and body language along with the words you are doing, and then pay attention to their nonverbal clues when they are talking.
- Listening and responding in a sensitive way to everything and not just good news or the nice things but also fear, sadness, embarrassment, and anger.
- Encourage them to talk and listen so that they can tell you how they are feeling.

Here are some tips that will help you listen and talk to your child:

Create some time to talk and listen to your child. They need to know that they can come to you whenever they need to. Anytime they have problems, have strong feelings, or just want to talk, give them your undivided attention.

Be open and talk about all sorts of things, including anxiety, fear, frustration, joy, and anger. When it comes to talking about feeling angry, it should be very different than if you are talking about getting angry. Understanding the difference between these two is an important step to help them learn how to communicate.

When it comes to talking with your child, you need to take a moment to remind yourself of when you were their age and how you liked it when others listened to what you had to say. Children and adults think very differently. There are a lot of things out there that children don't know and things they do know but don't have the right words to describe them.

You have to let your child finish their thought process before you respond. Even though they are a child, when you listen, avoid interrupting them, and definitely don't assume you know what they are trying to say. Even if they end up mispronouncing a word, saying some ridiculous, or struggle to find the right words, let them finish talking. Children are capable of appreciating this just like grownups do.

Use words that your child can understand. As adults, we tend to forget that kids don't understand everything that we do.

Watch their body language and facial expressions. When you listen to what they are saying, you don't just hear what they say but understand their words.

To let your child know that you are listening and that you want to understand what they are saying, you need to repeat what they said back to them and keep eye contact.

You can show them that you are interested in what they are saying by telling them something like, "Tell me more about...," "Really?" "Go on..." You should also ask them how they feel about the things that they are talking about.

NEVER blame or criticize them. If you feel yourself getting angry or upset about something that they did, try to explain why that action upset you. You need to get them to understand your position by appealing to their empathy.

You need to work with them to help them work through their conflicts and problems. You need to be totally honest with them so that they will be honest with you. If you make a point of learning how to listen and talk to your child from a very young age, you will have started a habit that will become increasingly useful when they become teens. You should want to have a relationship with your child where they feel comfortable talking to you about what they have done or who they are hanging out with. It will encourage them to talk to you about their life's various details as they get older.

Ten Strategies for Talking to Children

Everyone has heard about the "terrible twos." What causes this part of a child's developmental stage to seem so difficult to deal with? This time becomes such a challenge for parents because the toddler is trying to find the right type of balance between their dependence on their parents and autonomy. There are various opinions on how this behavior should be handled. But negotiating is a way to communicate that we could use with toddlers. We can model it with other adults, and this will teach our children ways to make sure that their needs are met while remaining respectful of others' needs.

While we've gotten to witness children showing concern for their crying friend, the perception they have of the world remains focused solely on what is around them at any given moment. Being sympathetic and sharing are skills that can end up taking them several years to master, and they to be encouraged to develop them, not forced.

Children are simply mirrors of their parents. They

can and will reflect back on everything they hear and see other adults do. Adults have to be aware of this and know that we are their role models. If you can begin with a respectful, open, and healthy relationship with your toddler, negotiating will become an opportunity to learn.

Below you will find a list of strategies you can use when negotiating with your child:

Your Child Has Their Own Way of Communicating

You have to know that your child has their own unique way they like to communicate. Is Timmy pulling Hannah's hair because he is frustrated with her? Is he learning that hair is actually attached to the head? Is he enjoying the power of making Hannah yell? Does he have words that he could use? Is this the first time that he has done these things, or has he done it before? This kind of information gives caregivers and parents a better perspective to help Timmy.

Know Your Emotions

You need to know your emotions and yourself. Adults and children experience the exact same feelings and needs. One of the best ways to model how to deal with these feelings and needs is by showing and telling them that we have the same feelings. You have to remember to remain calm and reassuring. These are some great ways to help negotiate with your child when they are excited or upset.

Be Authentic
This means that you have to be nonjudgmental, real, and honest during your interactions with your child. If we are respectful, our children will see that they are worthy of being respected just like other people.

Validate Their Feelings
It is fine for a child to feel frustrated, be scared, or cry. It could be beneficial to give their emotions labels. You could say something like, "Do you feel sad?" "Would you like to come to sit with me?" "You look like you really want that toy that Daniel is playing with." Most of the time, children just want adults to acknowledge their frustrations and to know that their feelings are being accepted. When we encourage our children to verbally express themselves verbally, we are helping them develop their language skills.

Address The Behavior
You need always to address the behavior and not the child if their behavior isn't appropriate. If your child is aggressive toward another child, you could say something like: "Hitting hurts. If you are angry with

Chris, you need to talk to her." This is better than saying things like: "You are bad. You know you aren't supposed to hit others!" You could use redirection as redirection might be helpful. If your child is running around their room, you could say: "It isn't safe to run inside. Do you want to go outside so we can run outside?"

Offer Choices

Give your child some choices if at all possible. Letting your child make choices empowers them and shows that you respect them. Asking your child: "Do you want me to change your diaper?" isn't a choice. You should try: "It is time to change your diaper. Would you like to choose your new diaper, or should I?"

Let Them Know About Transitions

If you give your child a five-minute warning before it is time for them to clean up, you are giving them time to finish their playtime before moving them to another activity. This gives them comfort and security, knowing what is going to happen next.

Explain Rules

You have to explain your rules to your child concisely and clearly. Young children feel secure when they have predictability. This means you have to give them clear guidelines and not have a lot of rules; the fewer, the better. Be consistent, prompt, and follow through with any consequences.

Give Time To Solve Problems

This area is a bit tricky. It is hard as a parent to watch our child struggle. The first thing we want to do is try to make things better for them. But being supportive and give your child time to work through their problems can help them a lot. Look for a smile to creep across their face when they figure out how to put that puzzle together, or they solve their social problem all by themselves. Self-confidence and learning are cultivated when people experience moderately stressful moments. These are going to be situations that challenge your child, but they should still be able to handle them.

Acknowledge Their Successes

You need to acknowledge their successes and efforts. Using positive reinforcements is very important to children. If you hear your child say: "I don't like that," rather than biting another child, you could say something like, "Denise, I heard you use your words. Way to go!" This can be very validating to a child.

This developmental stage is very challenging to a child and their parents. It can end up being a great time for both of you to explore the world with fascination. Their communication skills are blooming.

Their friendships are blossoming. Negotiation skills and communication styles are an important part of each of us. By supporting and helping this process in children, we are contributing to their emotional and social development and well-being.

Toddler Dictionary

Your toddler isn't made to ignore everything you say. They are still learning a language, so they don't understand words the way you and I do. We will go over some things that will help decode the toddler communication process to make discipline just a bit easier.

You Say: "Go To Your Room and Think About What you Did!"

When you say this, you likely mean something along the lines of, "I need to picture you marinating in your own guilt."

This tactic will not work for your toddler because it's a lot like telling your cat to think about what they did. Most toddlers aren't going to reflect on the things they did wrong in a meaningful way because there is a good chance that they don't fully understand what they did wrong.

You have to understand that your toddler will not ponder what they did and realize where they went wrong. However, you can teach them the right way of doing something. Children learn more by doing and watching than listening to you talk about the wrong and right things. We all know this, so why not use this information to help them. You need to model the behavior you want your child to do. For example, if your toddler doesn't' like sharing toys and snatches them away from their siblings, ensure they are there to see you spilt your apple slices with somebody at snack time. When they give you one of theirs, say "Thank you," and then you give them one of yours later. You may also want to try setting up a tea party using some toys and then ask them to practice sharing with the toys. When you start making good behavior a game, they will naturally start doing what you want.

You Say: "Be Gentle!"

When you say this, you likely want them to treat something gently. They could be bothering the cat, and you want them to stop.

The main reason why a toddler won't respond in this way is because they aren't sure what the word gentle meants. In addition to this, toddlers are just learning how to develop empathy. While they are starting to learning that other people have feelings, they are still pretty much egocentric. This means that they aren't going to be thinking about how the things they do affect others.

To say this in a way your child understands, encourage them to be understanding when they share how they feel. Try saying something like, "It hurts the cat when you pull their tail, just like it hurts when you fall." Then you should give them a specific command to show them the right way to do something. You could say, "This is how you should pet the cat," while holding their hand and using it to pet the cat gently. When you do this, you need to repeat the word gentle. This helps to illustrate what gentle actually means. Finally, you should give them a chance to do it for themselves. You should say, "Now show me gently," and then watch what they do.

You Say: "Do It Again, and You'll Get a Time-Out!"

When you say this, you likely mean, "can't you just listen and follow directions?" At that point, you are likely starting to feel like a broken record after asking them to stop doing something.

As for your toddler, what drives them to repeatedly do something even after you have told them to stop?

Well, it's not that they are purposefully ignoring what you are saying. That type of thing will come later on when they are teens. Toddlers and young children have yet to develop the ability to understand that when one thing happens, so can another. This means that the act of telling your toddler that something is going to happen if they continue doing something isn't going to sink in enough for them to stop what they are doing.

When it comes to a situation like this, it is easier if you don't say anything at all. The quickest way to fix this type of problem is to remove your child from the situation and get them focused on something different. If they are playing in the toilet, then you should redirect their attention. Gently pick them up, put them on the couch, and start doing something together, like reading, coloring, or doing a puzzle. This will stop the bad behavior, but over time, it will show them that certain things are bad.

You Say: "Don't Be Rude!"

When you say this, you likely mean that you want your child to show respect. A toddler isn't going to understand those words. As a toddler learns that what they say creates power for them, they are more likely to become defiant. Toddlers are going to talk to test your limits.

This is one of the first ways that they assert their independence. When you get a screaming "no," when you ask them to clean up their toys, this isn't because they want to make you mad or are trying to be a pain. They simply want to have some control in their life.

To get this point across, you can't take these things personally and snap whenever they challenge you. This is all just a necessary part of them becoming an adult. The best thing for a parent to do is show them the correct way to interact with others. You have to calmly say, "It's not okay to talk to me that way." Then you should empower them by offering them choices. You could reply with, "Would you like to put the books or blocks away first?" Once they receive some of the control they seek, they will be more likely to comply.

You Say: "Shh, Quiet!"

When you say this, you are likely trying to tell your child they need to be quiet. Maybe you are in the library with them, and you are mortified by how loud they are being. But, as soon as the words are out of your mouth, you find that your toddler doesn't do what you say.

Toddlers are still gaining control over how to control their voice and manage their impulses. Besides, social standards, like knowing when you are supposed to whisper, are going to take time to learn and internalize. You didn't know when you were supposed to whisper at their age.

When you want your toddler to be quiet, next time, try whispering, "Use this voice." Little kids love to copycat people, so if you show them how you want them to talk, they will follow suit. You need to take the time to practice speaking in "quiet voices" when you are at home. This will make things a lot easier if you give them a chance to move the behavior from on space where they feel safe, into a real-world situation. Finally, you have to tailor your expectations to your child's developmental stage. You have to expect that you are going to have to whisper reminders to them and take them out into the lobby often when you first visit a place that requires them to be quiet. When you do it this way, you are going to see the results you want.

CHAPTER 5: COMPASSION AND LOVE

CHAPTER 5: COMPASSION AND LOVE

Imagine this for a moment. Your child has a hard time getting organized and ready for school. You are both running late, and this isn't the first time this week that this has happened. Frustrated, you start yelling at them to hurry. It's an understandable reaction. Neither of you can afford to be late once more, and you know that your child needs to figure out how to manage their time wisely. However, when you react with frustration, the focus has been placed on your feelings and the child's experience. Through empathy, this dynamic can change. It gives you the chance to acknowledge the things you feel and see and what your child is going through.

This isn't the only place where empathy comes into play. If you claimed that we had an epidemic of bullying in our society, you would be right because of the number of accounts from children where they were bullied. The issue here is not the bullying action, though that is troubling. The major issue is that most of the children in our society lack an understanding of compassionate behavior.

Humans have a basic need to belong. Prosocial behaviors are learned through connections with other people. Developing empathic abilities begin right at birth.

Empathy provides you a way to connect. It shows your child that you understand they are going through something, even if you don't fully understand their feelings. Empathy lets them know that they're not alone.

This is a very important message for your child. When a child feels supported and understood, they will stay motivated. Empathy should not be confused for sympathy. Sympathy means you feel sorry for them. Sympathy means you feel bad for your child. Sympathy can end up causing you to lower your expectations. To be empathetic means that you don't lower your expectations. It allows you to validate how they feel and keep your standards where they are. When you connect with them and show empathy, you can prove to them that you believe they are capable and strong.

People have been studying empathy for a long time, and yet it still remains confused when viewed through the lens of moral behavior and social justice. We have discovered an intersection between psychology, neuroscience, and moral decision making. Through empathic parental care, humans will learn to think about things from others' perspective because they have learned how to do it and are mirroring others' actions.

When a child lacks empathic abilities, numerous self-criticizing behaviors show up, which will cause more emotional and psychological harm.

Empathy is made up of four main elements:

1. Looking at things from their perspective, you have to put your own reactions and feelings aside to see things from their viewpoints.
2. Get rid of judgment – Step back from what is go-

ing on and stop yourself from jumping to conclusions about what is happening.
3. Understand how they are feeling – Tap into what your child is experiencing to figure out how they actually feel. Think back to your moment in life when you felt that way. Ensure you don't overdo this, though. Children have their own experiences.
4. Let them know you understand – Allow your kid to express how they feel without jumping it to try and fix things. Avoid using various phrases like, "what you need to do is." Instead, you need to say something like, "It sounds like you," or "I hear that you."

While empathy may not be about feeling sorry for them, it is focused on feelings. When you ensure that you are responding with empathy, it means you fully understand that your child is going through something. This includes the challenges they are facing and how it is affecting their emotions. It's easy for parents to assume that they know what has upset their child. For example, if they like to hide when a family member comes over, you could find yourself thinking they are rude. In reality, they could be feeling overwhelmed by the extra people and wanting to find a quiet moment.

When you tune into your child's emotions, it shows them that you accept and understand them. It helps families talk about their actions. It is also important that you learn to acknowledge your own emotions. The things that are happening with your child in moments of stress will have an emotional impact on you. It's difficult for you to show empathy when you are feeling angry or frustrated. It is okay to take a moment for yourself before you say anything.

When you're ready to show empathy, it lets them know that you are trying to move beyond how you feel to understand what your child is going through. They also get to see you model healthy self-control, which helps teach them how to manage their emotions effectively.

Compassion for Kids

Defining what compassion for children is can be quite hard if you try to explain things in adult terms. Telling a child that compassion is "a sympathetic consciousness of others' distress together with a desire to alleviate it" is going to go right over their heads, and all you're going to get is a blank stare. Kids have to have definitions in words that they are going to understand. One of the first steps in understanding how they understand compassion is to ask them to define these words:

- Generosity
- Benevolence
- Understanding
- Humanity
- Kindness
- Empathy
- Mercy
- Sensitivity
- Philanthropy
- Condolence

If your child defines one of the words, relate the definition they give you to compassion. When you help them understand the vocabulary of the need to help others in distress, it will deepen their understanding of compassion. Helping your child take others' perspective is an important step in assisting them in understanding compassion.

Children will develop different levels of empathy at various ages. This development of empathy is a necessity for compassion. That's why you need to start developing compassion from birth. During their first year of life, a child develops global empathy. They will start matching the emotions that they see.

When a parent picks up their child and helps soothe them by singing to them, the child will calm and react to those facial expressions. The child learns compassion during these foundational interactions.

Kids Absorb Emotions

Parents may notice that their children, especially when they are toddlers, go from a sweet little child to a grumpy one. They start to wonder what happened to the sweet child they use to have. That sweetness hasn't gone anywhere, but as they get older, they develop the ability to mirror others' behaviors and interpret those actions. They also learn how to recognize they have needs and that they want those needs filled.

While this may sound rather cynical, the more children learn how the world doesn't always reward being kind, and they are less likely to be the sweet kid you once knew. When they see you cut off somebody while taking them to school or not holding the door open for another person to walk through, they notice it. They are learning that if they act in their own self-interest, they have a better chance of getting what they want.

We all have a part in our brain known as the amygdala. This is the part of the brain that regulates self-control. If a bear is chasing you, it is the part of your brain that tells you to fight or run. As a young child, this part is underdeveloped, so they don't have self-control. In children who haven't received proper nurturing, the amygdala is stuck in the "on" position.

When it's always on, hormones like cortisol, norepinephrine, and epinephrine are constantly being released. These were all very helpful for our ancestors from thousands of years ago when things with large, sharp teeth were chasing them. However, as it turns out, in the 21st Century, this can greatly impact our wellness and health. When kids are always in this state, it doesn't give them the chance to be calm, think things through, and see the different solutions. The only thing they are trying to do is survive.

Fortunately, the brain will get better at dealing with problems. Part of this is due to your influence and making sure you are a good role model for them. You can do this through love, compassion, and empathy. However, the majority of the changes are all on them. The brain does not fully mature and develop until our mid-20s, and even then, something might not be fully developed. There are programs in school, though, that promote emotional intelligence and meditation. Children between the ages of five and seven have shown a strong ability to understand compassion and empathy. While children will naturally be immature, it doesn't mean they are unreachable.

The Growth of Empathy In Kids

When you show your child empathy, you are teaching them empathy. A two-year-old can try to make an upset friend feel better by giving them a blanket or pacifier. They likely don't understand why the child is crying, but they remember times when they have felt sad and knows what made them feel better. By three, children are much more aware of others, but they can't fully relate to how other people feel. They could find it fun to knock down a block tower and not understanding why that child starts crying.

By four, children have a stronger understanding about hurting a person and may start to give apologies without having somebody tell them to. They tend to be quite empathetic about injuries to another child. Once they reach age five or six, they share better and should know how to take turns with things. They can also discuss what it means to be kind and help come up with ideas of how they can help people.

So, have you hugged your child today? For children who don't get enough love in their home, their empathy will suffer. This is true for those who have parents who focus on their child to be good enough. When children are told they didn't do enough when they came in second, they will struggle with empathy and self-compassion. When a child doesn't receive compassion and empathy from their parent, they will have a hard time developing relationships independently.

We are going to go through some ways to ensure you teach your child about being compassionate and goodhearted.

1. Believe that they are always capable of being kind – If you are constantly treating your child like they are getting into trouble, they are going to start acting badly eventually. However, when you assume that they are concerned for people and want to do good, they are going to that.
2. Show them positive actions – The things you say and do around your child has a huge impact on them. You want your kids to see you being kind to people, like helping a friend in need. Most parents will begin this role-modeling from

day one. This will help to create a strong foundation for a lifetime of openness with people and give-and-take.
3. Treat them with respect – Respect for a child can be as simple as letting them know that playtime is nearly over. Just yanking your kid away from playing because you suddenly realize you need to leave is disrespectful. You wouldn't do that to an adult, so why do that to a child. It can also help if you point out healthy conflict resolution with real experiences. You could say something like, "Mommy and Daddy don't always agree on things, but we always listen to each other and treat each other with respect instead of putting each other down."
4. Teach them how to notice facial expressions – Learning other people's perspectives can be done through reading their nonverbal language. People are more likely to help a person in need when they can imagine how the world looks from their point of view.
5. Let them know that how they treat people matters – Children may think it's funny to see a person get splashed by water when a car goes by. You could point out the fact that the woman wasn't laughing at what happened to them. "Look at her face; she looks sad."
6. Don't let rudeness go – If a cashier was particularly grumpy, you could say something to your

child like, "Wow, they must have been having a bad day to talk in such a mean voice. What do you think?" This will let your child know that when somebody is nasty to them, that they don't have to be mean in response.

7. Acknowledge kindness – On the flip side of things, you need to acknowledge when people do kind things. If a person slows down to let you out, you could say, "It was nice of that driver to let me out." When your child does something nice, you need to know to acknowledge what they did and praise them.

8. Understand your perceives people differently – Young children will notice differences in others just like they notice them in colors of crayons and animals, so assume the best. If they end up saying something socially inappropriate, you need to explore the comment calmly. Ask them why they would say that. Then you correct what they said and explain things to them.

9. Be sensitive to messages that they learn from media – Kids can imitate the good actions that they see in the media or read about just like they will act out other things. Ensure you know what they are watching and be there if they need to talk about what they saw. You should encourage them to read books that focus on compassion and caring.

10. Explain that excluding people from play or call-

ing them names hurts as much as hitting – If you ever hear your child call another child a name, you need to go into a problem-solving mode with both of the children. Point out that the child who was made fun of is upset. Then you need to recognize the real problem, which could be that the name-caller wants the toy that the other kid has. Ask, "If you want something, what would be another way to get it without making them feel bad?" You also need to make sure the child called a name doesn't feel victimized and encourages your child to apologize to them.
11. Avoid creating competition in the family – While saying something like, "Let's see who can clean up the fastest," may seem like it would motivate them, it risks causing your children to become rivals. When you pit one child against the other, they are taught to view people as obstacles. This is going to create problems when they need to work with people. Instead, please encourage them to help each other clean up and praise the group's effort.
12. Show them how to help people – Encourage your children to donate toys that they have outgrown. You can also get them involved in making cookies or other treats to take to shelters, and then they can come with you to take things to those in the hospital.

13. Be patient – Compassion and kindness are learned and life will present us with challenges. Simply being a good role model and a loving parent goes a long way towards making sure that your raise a tolerant, wonderful human being.

Even if you believe that you are doing everything right, or if you feel you have messed up, you can only influence so much in your child's life. If you are a kind person in general, and you are here reading this, then you probably don't have much to worry about, and everything will work out just fine.

VI

CHAPTER 6: REMAINING CALM WHEN YOU DON'T THINK YOU CAN

CHAPTER 6: REMAINING CALM WHEN YOU DON'T THINK YOU CAN

Let's be honest, with a child-parent relationship; you have one person with mature self-control and one with less self-control. This means that parents not only have to regulate their emotions, but they have to help their kids regulate theirs. Kids are uncivilized, not by choice but by design. They don't understand social rules about expressing emotions. One of the main tasks as a parent is to teach children how to express themselves, so they honor their emotions in a healthy way.

Depending on their age, what is happening in their life, and their temperament, kids aren't well-equipped to handle frustration, disappointment, how to focus, evaluate options, make good decisions, or calm down. But how well-equipped are we? What did we do in our lives before having children to get us ready to handle a being with little self-control?

If you are like most parents, the answer is not much. This is likely why people say that you can never be fully prepared for having a child. Before you become a parent, you don't know what it is like to be completely responsible for a tiny human, to put their needs before yours, and to always be thinking of them.

However, it could be that we have been preparing our entire lives for this moment. Our system of self-regulation has been highly influenced by our childhood and what we have experienced in life. Some are more regulated than users by nature, some became regulated by experience, but all of us will need to do a bit of work on ourselves and adapt to having a child.

Then we have the fun of continuing to adapt. As

they grow, we grow with them, but outgrowth is internal.

We talk about how important it is to teach children self-regulation, but what do we do about our own? How can we develop those skills? How can you teach your child to handle their frustration when you have a hard time handling yours?

What's funny is our children know how to hone in on what we need to work on. They can push buttons like nobody else. They are Jedi Masters that can expose weak spots. We have to take the challenge and be mindful. Here are some ways to help you remain calm even when you don't think you can.

Tips to Help You Remain Cool When Your Child Misbehaves

Every parent is going to get angry at their child from time to time. There isn't anything wrong with anger; anger is an emotion that holds a message. The problem happens when we can't hear the message when we are angry. During the heat of the moment, we are in the freeze, flight, or flight mode. If we hit the "fight mode," our child is going to look like an enemy. So, we think the message tells us to get rid of our enemy, our child.

But, the message when your child is upset is that they need your help, even if they are being impossible. We might need to put them to bed earlier than their normal time. You might want to connect with them more. You just want to make it safe enough for them to cry and show those fears and tears that are causing them to act out. You won't be able to understand or act on this message when we get triggered by our own anger and fear. Remaining cool is needed actually to solve the problem rather than making it worse.

How in the world can you remain cool when your child is acting out rather than sliding into the darkness?

1. Realize That You Are Getting Annoyed

There might be times when we don't realize until too late that we have moved into the darkness. Normally you can feel your annoyance building when you begin gathering kindling. What does that mean? You begin looking at all reasons why you are right, and your child is being an ungrateful brat. When you begin gathering kindling, it will be hard to stay away from a fire. As soon as you realize that the chatter in your mind is about your child being negative, you have to STOP. Stop whatever you are doing. Take some deep breaths to stop the anger train.

1. Hit The Pause Button

Even if you have gone down the wrong path and you are yelling at your child. Just STOP. Take a few deep breaths and hit pause. Just shut your mouth even if you are in the middle of a sentence. You don't need to feel embarrassed because you are showing good anger management skills. Save the embarrassment for another time.

1. Take A Break

Never try to address a problem with your child while you are angry. Take the time and calm down. Get yourself re-centered so you can hear the anger's message. Did your child's behavior scare you? Do you feel resentment toward your partner? Are you stressed out and exhausted so that you over-react to your child's appropriate behavior?

1. Feel Your Body's Emotions

I'm not saying you have to swallow your anger. You just need to not react to it. Notice your body's anger. Feel it tighten in your stomach; feel your throat constricting and suffocating you. Breathe into these places. While you open up to those feelings, you are going to feel them start to change and melt away. This is the secret to being mindful. When you are able to sit with your emotions and accept them, they will melt away.

1. Change Your State

Now you need to reframe your thoughts about the situation to make new feelings. If you think your child needs to be taught a lesson right this minute, you are going to be too angry. If you can remind yourself that they are just acting like a child since they are a child and they need your love more when it seems like they deserve it the least, you will be willing to change your anger.

1. Go For A Do-Over

You need to admit to your child that you got upset and that you are sorry. Tell them that both of you are going to go for a do-over. You have to stay calm this time and empathize with your child. Listen to their feelings and see things from their point of view. NEVER blame them and try to find solutions that will work for each of you. If your child broke something, ask them what they could do to fix it. Always begin by listening to them and empathizing with them.

1. Practice

I will not lie to you. Parenting is hard work, and it will be the hardest job you ever have in your life. If you normally fly off the handle, you are going to have to teach your brain new ways to self-discipline. This is going to take a lot of practice. The good news is that you are rewiring your brain each time you resist acting out when you get angry. This means that managing your anger will get easier each time you do it.

1. Reframe Expectations

Like with everything we have learned in this book, it isn't something that you can only do once. This is partly because of the fact that your child is constantly changing, and your expectations are going to change. Any parent can end up expecting too much from their child. It is easy to do. Remind yourself on a regular basis that they are a child. You can expect them to act overexcited, out of control, and impulsive.

Sometimes a child's physical and cognitive development doesn't match up to their emotional and social development. That's fine, and that is normal.

Where ever they are developmentally is where they are.

Parents can help them to develop, but sometimes you have to accept where they. Children are more emotional than adults. Constantly remind yourself that self-control skills don't become organized until the age of three and won't mature until around five or six. There is continuously changed to this in childhood, and a major growth will happen during adolescence. There are some estimates that state final maturation doesn't occur until age 30.

Too often, kids get punished for being humans. They aren't allowed to be grumpy, have bad days, a bad attitude, or a disrespectful tone, yet as adults, we do it all the time. We believe if we don't nip these things in the bud, it can escalate, and we lost control. You have to release the unfounded fear and allow them just to be human.

1. Separate Their Emotions from Yours

Just because your child is rather emotional doesn't mean you have to be. Their emotions and your emotions aren't connected. This sounds so simple, yet it's difficult to do. We have been taught that the way our children act is a reflection of us, and if they act out, then we must be bad parents. If you believe that, please go reread the previous chapter. Kids have meltdowns and act out sometimes; it's a normal emotional response when they are a toddler.

When kids act crazy, it triggers a stress response. However, with practice, you can remain calm. You can learn how to respond instead of reacting to what they are doing. When you learn how to do this, it becomes much easier for them to cope.

1. Take Care of Yourself

Being well-rested is another big factor in staying calm. When you are rested, you are more prepared to face problems. However, it's more common to be overtired as a parent as opposed to being well-rested. Being able to remain calm also takes a toll on the body, and when you have nothing to give, it can be vertically impossible to remain calm.

You need to learn to take a break when you need it. This can be hard for modern moms. You need to work some self-care breaks into your day. Find joy in the mundane moments in your day. Take time for yourself and be a little easier on yourself.

Even if you stick to these tips, there will come a

time when you will lose them. It happens. You are at your wit's end, and they do that one thing, and you scream. Losing it is part of life. It can even be a learning moment for your child. You can lose it, but show your child the correct way to respond. First, admit that you lost your temper or got upset. Second, apologize for what you may have said or done because parents do make mistakes. Three, tell your child what you did to calm down. This is a journey.

You will lose it every now and then, but if you continue to practice, hold yourself with compassion, and notice your emotions, you will find that anytime your child acts out, you will be able to remain cool. There will come a time when you notice that you hardly ever lose your temper anymore. You are still going to have childish behaviors as long as you have children, but the way you react is going to be different. There won't be as much drama but there will be a lot of love.

VII

CHAPTER 7: SCHOOL

CHAPTER 7: SCHOOL

It isn't unusual for children to behave in different ways in different settings. You might expect your child to act a certain way at a birthday party and another way at their grandparent's house. But a child's behavior, particularly ones that have problems like autism, SDHD, learning disabilities, and anxiety, can be different, especially when a child is at home or at school. These discrepancies might leave parents a bit perplexed and worried that they are doing things wrong.

Let's look at Sam; he is 15, very smart but has been diagnosed with ADHD, autism spectrum disorder, and some learning challenges. His mother, who is an executive director at "Twice Exceptional Children's Advocacy" remembers how school challenges caused some explosive behaviors when he was at home.

When he was at school, he was constantly trying to interact with classmates while trying to please his teachers. He was working extremely hard to control himself. When he finally got home, he was looking for ways to get rid of all that built-up tension. When he finally released it, it was by throwing a 30-minute tantrum. He would butt his head against the way, kicked, screamed, threw things, etc. Once he finally calmed down, he would be full of guilt and shame.

For many children, school is the place where they are met with their biggest challenges. Let's look at Chloe; she is eight and has been diagnosed with social anxiety and selective mutism. Her mother says she is an energetic, talkative, goofy, and fun little girl. When she goes to school, she completely shuts down. She has never been about to speak to her classmates or teachers, even though she participates in every area that doesn't require her to be verbal. She never asks to go to the restroom. She will hold herself until she gets home.

Why do some children perform very differently in various places?

Why Certain Children Perform Better

Some children might do fine meeting all their school's expectations, but it is a huge struggle for them, and it will take a toll on them at home. Children who have learning disabilities, autism, anxiety, and ADHD might have to use their resources just to be able to cope or follow directions in the classroom. When the child gets home, it is hard for them to come up with the same resources to be able to manage.

Most children who are on the autism spectrum do benefit from having a routine, predictability, structure, and consistency that comes within a classroom environment. This sometimes can't be done at home since this isn't how life actually works.

When a child is at school, consequences and rewards will happen consistently that might be challenging for parents to create at home. Social modeling at school might help a child stay in line. Plus, teachers don't have time for dawdling. If a child doesn't follow their directions on the first or even second attempt, the teacher is going to have some immediate consequences. Parents tend to let their child delay or avoid doing the next thing since they take too much time just talking about it.

Suppressing Symptoms

Children who have certain disorders like OCD or anxiety are extremely concerned about how other people see them, especially once they get into middle and high school. They try extremely hard to hide any of their symptoms. Normally, we see children functioning at higher levels when in school. They aren't as symptomatic since they are trying to keep up a perception that they are fine. They normally feel shameful or embarrassed about their symptoms.

Another reason children do better when in school is because they feel safe to be "their worst selves" when they are home. They know that their parents are still going to support and love them.

Children come home, and they feel relieved. It is like a female coming home and taking off their heels and bra. They think, "great, and now I can just be myself." For any child who has kept their symptoms suppressed during school when they get home, they don't feel like anybody is judging them. This is why you might see their symptoms explode.

One mother who had a ten-year-old OCD child said her daughter would doodle or rock herself to try and stop their obsessive thoughts. Although she was feeling stressed, she knew she had to bottle it up while in school, and once she stepped off the bus, she would explode. Verbally and physically, she was extremely upset.

This can cause parents to be very confused, too. It

is common for a parent to say, "I take to your teachers and they all tell me that you are great in class and that you don't squirm or act out. Why can't I see any of these things at home?" The child gets home and they are very symptomatic, and they have a hard time keeping it under control.

Why Some Do Better At Home

For many children, social and academic demands during school are beyond anything they face when they are at home. This might trigger some problem behaviors that their parents don't see.

Children who have problems like anxiety and ADHD usually have an extremely low tolerance for frustration. When you ask them to either be persistent or patient during school could stress them out. This is very challenging for a child. This might cause them to act out in these situations.

Children who have social anxiety might worry about what other people think about them. Children who have performance anxiety may not have any problems when they are at home. Once they get to school and are asked to read something out loud or do the math that they don't completely understand, they might act out somehow, so they don't have to do the assignment. Acting out might be functional for them since their teacher might scold them when they act out, but they move on.

If a child is autistic, they might be allowed to act a certain way at home, like playing with Legos or having some screen time. When they are in school, they don't get to do these things or have a hard time waiting for an activity to open up to do it. This could cause some disruptive behaviors too.

How Can You Help

The best suggestion is to encourage open communication and collaboration between school and home as often as you can. If there are some techniques or strategies that the child does at school or home, could these be adapted and shared to help the child in both environments?

If it helps a child to have a schedule they can see while in school, could the parents create one for the home? If you know that your child benefits from "when/then" statements when at home, this means you would say, "when you do this, then this is going to happen" you can share this with their teacher so they can use it too.

The best way to have the best relationship with your child's school is to praise their teacher and value the work that they do while giving them information about the child.

For a child who acts out at home, give the child a chance to decompress after they get home. It is fine to be a bit "loose, goosy" with the rules during this time if your child needs to take a break. But they still know that the house rules need to be followed.

You need to notice how nourished and rested your child is. If they come home hungry after they have struggled all day to stay calm, this is a disaster waiting to happen. Give them a snack and let them rest. Give them the time to regroup so they can have a good start to their evening.

Therapy Might Help
The best tool that many experts recommend to help children manage their behavior is CBT or cognitive behavioral therapy. This therapy has been adapted for various behavioral and emotional challenges. These therapies help children learn how to regulate themselves and ways to handle any powerful emotions better than acting impulsively.

If a child used their CBT skills during school, they would be able to function better without having to use a lot of energy. Once they get home, they won't be as stressed and won't have an explosion. The more they can practice these skills, the better they will get.

When using CBT, parents are included in the therapy from the start so they can understand their child's condition so they can understand what they have been doing that might have contributed to the problem. Therapists can teach the parents all the dos and don'ts about ways to be a parent to a child who has anxiety disorders. If you are a parent to a child who has OCD and is a germaphobe, you aren't doing them any good if you just open doors for them. They have to learn the skills that can help them deal with their compulsions and anxieties.

Behavioral parent training does include some CBT that can help parents figure out what is happening in their child's environment so they can support them.

Teachers and Parents Need to Work Together

If you want your child to have success at school, you have to make sure that you and their teacher are working together. This can be a bit tough at times, and it might seem like there is a line that has been drawn down the center of your child's life.

There are things you know about your child; you know how you help them get through their homework and how they play with their siblings. At school, there are the things that their teacher knows about them that help them get their school work done while interacting with their peers.

All this information from both sides needs to be combined to understand the child better. This isn't just going to benefit the child but will help their teacher and you, the parent. Look at the tips below to create a good relationship with their teacher.

Communication

This is something that parents hear all the time, but it needs to be repeated often. The main key for teachers and parents to work together better is through communication. What might not always be so clear is that communication does work both ways.

Yes, there are several things that you need to tell their teacher at the beginning of the school year to start their year off on the right foot. The responsibility for keeping up that teacher/parent relations doesn't rely just on the parent.

This relationship will only work if their teacher puts in an effort to respond to your questions and concerns but shares their compliments and concerns with you.

Teachers and parents have one common goal. They both want to create the best education they can for the child. If teachers and parents can work together, they will be able to move toward this common goal. There are loads of new technology out there that is making communication between parents and teachers so much easier. It has improved the quality and quantity of communication. Teachers and parents need to find every opportunity to communicate with each other regularly to make sure that every child has their intellectual, emotional, and physical needs met. You will see the best educational outcomes when you ensure the needs have been met.

What do you do if you think their teacher isn't doing their part?

Approach Their Problems

Handling a difficult teacher is going to be hard, but it isn't as uncommon as you might think. If you think your child's teacher isn't sharing information or is being completely unfair to your child, it is time to have a conference with that teacher and ask them what is happening.

Remember that to get the most from your time; it is important to schedule a meeting before going to the school. You can't find them at a school function and confront them either. You wouldn't want their teacher to come to the park and face you on the weekend.

Partnerships

Having a partnership implies that every party is working together. They will treat one another as equals who have certain responsibilities and rights to reach a common goal. Every party makes sure that they share their knowledge and skills towards meeting the objective. The bad news is that a lot of this communication goes one-sided. They may share the information, but their power isn't. When this happens, it isn't creating a real partnership. Most of the crises at home or school are caused by poor communication.

In the beginning, teachers have to create credibility as being confident and competent professionals. They have to set a tone for collaboration and give certain responsibilities, roles, and goals to every partnership member.

To maintain this stage, teachers have to use communication and conferencing to enhance and continue this partnership.

The end-stage will bring the right closure by coming up with a well thought out transition for the next academic step for the child. This will give the child the best outcome that they can reach at the moment. Teachers should encourage the family as they take on this next step.

This last stage could be hard for parents and teachers on specific academic levels. If the child is very young, parents usually depend on the teacher and don't want this relationship to end. Teachers have to communicate with parents asking them to talk to the child's next teacher, and they will also step in and help with this transitional phase.

Handling the Tough Things Together

Every child is not going to have an easy transition when going to school, and they might not enjoy being at school. They have estimated that about five percent of all children who go to school show some signs of "school refusal behaviors" at some point in their lives. Every day many children complain about being bored.

Some parents will shoulder the responsibility and blame their children's problems and don't talk to the school since they feel like it is their problem to handle. Some parents might feel like the school is judging them when they get a call asking them to talk about their child. This isn't always the case. In most situations, sitting down and working out some solutions together is the best way to handle the harder situations.

Handling "school refusal" is going to require you and the schools to talk about everything you know about your child and use that information to find a plan to get them into the classroom.

Finding the reasons behind why your child is bored at school needs to be done together. Listening to what your child tells you at home can help the school. Knowing the things that have been said and done in the classroom will give you some context you can use when listening to your child's complaints.

Parents or teachers shouldn't ever get argumentative or defensive with one another if they are faced with challenging situations. Never try to construct a defense with numerous rationales or excuses. This approach will only bring about anger and will weaken the partnership.

Just apologize for any errors and tell them you regret the situation that happened. Give them some steps that you will take to keep this from happening again. A person who is extremely upset will respond to an apology. Apologizing sincerely isn't showing weakness or incompetence. They are actually signs of confidence and strength.

To have an effective, functioning partnership, the power has to be equally shared. When in a parent-teacher partnership, you have to stay mindful that each party will have unique skills and knowledge. Parents are going to know their child's developmental history, lifestyle, and interests. Teachers will have knowledge of assessing strategies, school procedures, school policies, teaching, and how well the student is performing. Teachers and parents need to learn how to share the knowledge to help everybody involved.

What teachers have learned about a student can be very powerful for the child while they work with them at home. It's also important that parents keep a positive dialogue with their children when talking about school. Parents have to be interested in the child's schoolwork. Parents have to look at their child's assignments. Parents have to make sure that they praise their child's efforts, establish a place and time for their homework, foster independence, and give them chances to learn at home through activities and games. You need to make sure the child has a supportive and warm home environment. Don't show disappointment or punish your child. Always nurture and encourage your child's relationships with their peers.

Think About Other Perspectives

Creating a partnership between teachers and parents could rely on the teachers listening to what the parents have to say and the parents taking time to understand where the teacher is coming from. There might be a time when teachers and parents are both guilty of dismissing the other person's viewpoint.

The more a parent feels dismissed, the less they

are going to participate in their child's education. If a teacher feels like they aren't being heard, they might stop communicating altogether.

Things that might seem a bit confrontational, such as an outline of the type of homework, help their teachers what the parent to do, or the parent telling the school what they need to do to accommodate their child's allergies. These things might not be as demanding as they seem. The end goal is going to be the same for both the school and parent... they want to help their child be successful, safe, and responsible.

Research has shown that students who are too stressed can't learn well because their bodies are releasing the stress hormone called cortisol that hinders memories from forming. If the student's school and home environments are calm, their brain can learn a lot better. This is why it is important to make a support system that is strong for them at school and home to help them learn better. The best way to do this is to make sure this happens through regularly communicating things between school and home. Parents can call the teacher or send an email if they think the home environment is holding their child back. If the child is sick or trying to deal with the death of somebody close to them, sending their teacher a quick email to let them know that the child is having a hard time might make it easier on the student and teacher. Teachers also need to tell the parents if any problems come up at school like new stressors, changes in their behavior, or their schoolwork goes down. The teacher could call or send an email to the parents so that they can work together to figure out if the child needs some more support.

If teachers and parents work together as a team, they can create the best environment to make an intellectual, emotional, and physically well-rounded student.

VIII

CONCLUSION

CONCLUSION

I would like to thank you once more for reading this book. I hope that everything has been informative and able to give you new insights into positive discipline. I hope that you found the information helpful, as well, and can help you for years to come as your raise your children to be amazing adults.

Parenting is rewarding and tough all at the same time. While you can't know what kind of adult your child will be until they are out of your hands, you can rest easy at night knowing you have done your best. The most important thing is to make sure you don't focus too much on everything that your child does wrong. Ensure your child knows when they do something you approve of so that they know how they should behave. You can't expect them to read your mind, just like you can't read theirs, and that's why communication is the most important factor when it comes to parenting. Bad communication tends to be what lies behind all big problems. If there is only one thing you take away from this book, I hope it fills in those communication gaps. I feel that will serve you the most. Above all, get to know your child and appreciate them for the individual person they are.

Lastly, I would like to ask that if you found this book helpful in any way, please leave a review on Amazon! Thanks!

www.ingramcontent.com/pod-product-compliance
Ingram Content Group UK Ltd.
Pitfield, Milton Keynes, MK11 3LW, UK
UKHW022210230426
12048UKWH00016BA/766